7 DAYS

IN THE BEGINNING GOD CREATED

Original content written by a panel of Christian authors.
Compiled and edited by Jonathan Rice.

Illustrated by Mary Ann Zapalac - www.zapalacart.com

This booklet has been written to help Christians of any age to understand more about the world around them, as created by God around 6,000 years ago.

It has been carefully designed to explain complex principles from both Science and the Scriptures in a way that can be simply understood.

It also clearly presents the Lord Jesus Christ, the Son of God, as the only one who can save sinners from eternal punishment by His own death and resurrection.

But these are written, that ye might believe that Jesus is the Christ, the Son of God; and that believing ye might have life through His name.

John 20:31

Copyright © Scripture Teaching Library and Jonathan Rice, 2014.
ISBN: 978-1-909789-21-0

All rights reserved. Excerpts from this publication may be used for teaching purposes, however the whole publication may not be reproduced, stored in or introduced into a retrieval system, or transmitted, in any form or by any means (electronic, mechanical, photocopying, recording or otherwise), without the prior written permission of the copyright owner.

Published by
SCRIPTURE TEACHING LIBRARY
Cookstown, Northern Ireland.
www.scriptureteachinglibrary.com

Printed by Kingsbridge Press Ltd, Cookstown, Northern Ireland.

CONTENTS

Introduction 2

Day One 4

Day Two 8

Day Three 12

Day Four 16

Day Five 20

Day Six 24

Day Seven 28

INTRODUCTION

> In the beginning God created the heaven and the earth. And the earth was without form, and void; and darkness was upon the face of the deep. And the Spirit of God moved upon the face of the waters.
>
> Genesis 1: 1-2

The beginning of the universe, the 'evolution' of life and the extinction of the dinosaurs are subjects that have been debated for many years. Yet in the first words of the first book of the Bible we discover the truth from the very beginning of time.

In the beginning God created...

In His first act of creation, even before the universe began, the eternal God of heaven created time. Before the opening verse of Genesis chapter 1, time did not exist. There was no beginning, and there was no end. Time was to become the container into which God would place His created universe (*the heaven*) and our home (*the earth*).

Immediately after this act of creation, the earth was in complete darkness, and although the Spirit of God was near, there was no light to show the glory of God. The earth had no characteristics, no detail, no beauty and yet it was here that God chose to display His power through creation.

In a similar way, the Bible tells us that every person is born spiritually dark, in sin, without the light of God in their heart. That sin, which separates us from the holy God of heaven, destroys our character, our beauty and our future. That sin makes us undesirable to God, deserving only the punishment of hell. However, just as God chose this dark, empty planet to perform a work of awesome power, so He has chosen the dark hearts of men, women, boys and girls to perform the mighty work of redemption. Through this He brings us back to Himself, shining the light of the Gospel into our hearts.

God was not alone at the beginning. In Genesis 1:1 when we read the word 'God', it is the original Hebrew word 'Elohiym', a plural word, and the name for the Trinity of God the Father, God the Son and God the Holy Spirit. It was God the Son, Jesus Christ, who was sent from heaven to bring us back to God.

> Around 400BC, the Ancient Greeks said for the 'first' time that Earth may be round instead of flat. 400 years before, Isaiah 40:22 said that Earth was a circle. The Bible, God's Word, was right all along.

Coming down to a sinful earth, leaving the glory of heaven, Jesus lived a perfect life, only to take the punishment for our sins when He shed His precious blood at Calvary. It is only through this blood and His resurrection that we can be brought back to God. Everything that we see in nature points us towards this truth and the gift of salvation that is freely offered to us.

In this booklet we will consider God's eye-witness account of His own creation. A creation that, according to the generations recorded in the Bible, took place only 6,000 years ago. It is our desire that as you read this booklet you will see that this suggestion, though publicly ridiculed from the viewpoint of evolution, is in perfect agreement with science.

Although the theories of man often dismiss the account of the Bible, observed science will never conflict with Scripture. As Galileo, Copernicus, Newton, Faraday and Einstein all found: a greater understanding of one can lead to a fuller experience of the other.

DAY ONE

> And God said, Let there be light: and there was light. And God saw the light, that it was good: and God divided the light from the darkness. And God called the light Day, and the darkness He called Night. And the evening and the morning were the first day.
>
> Genesis 1: 3-5

Travelling at a speed of 670 million miles per hour, passing straight through solid objects and almost always invisible, electromagnetic radiation plays a leading role in practically every waking moment of our lives.

This radiation exists in the form of the radio and television waves that carry our favourite channels, the infrared signals coming from the remote control and the microwaves that heat our food. We also have ultraviolet rays for scanning bank-notes, x-rays for checking our bodies, and high-energy gamma rays.

However, it is the visible part of the electromagnetic spectrum that we simply could not live without, and for that reason, on the very first day of creation, God created light.

This light, a vital resource in our day-to-day lives, is given a very special place throughout the Bible. In Genesis chapter 1, the light is called 'good', which describes the character of the Creator. In 1 John 1:5 we read that 'God is light', and in John 8:12, Jesus Christ, the Son of God said 'I am the light of the world'.

So what is light, what are its properties and what can it tell us about God the Father, and the Lord Jesus Christ?

Light is all around us. A light, switched on in a dark room, will immediately fill the entire room with light, just as the presence of God is all around us. God sees everything we do and think, even when no-one else is around.

Light is real. Although we can't actually see the rays of light passing in front of our eyes, we know they exist, because we see the light reflecting off the objects in front of us. God's creation reflects the invisible presence of God. The trees, the birds, all the wonderful colours of creation, the rain and the snow all reflect the glory of God's creation and prove that He is real.

Light moves at great speed. Covering a distance of 50,000 miles in the time it takes you to blink, a ray of light could travel around the world 7.5 times in one second! Many people wonder how God can hear and answer so many prayers at one time; how God can constantly care for so many of His people. But a God who can create light doesn't live with the same restrictions that we do. It is nothing for a God like that to be in every place at the same time.

Light can be 'scattered'. A rainbow, the symbol of God's promise to Noah in Genesis 9, is an example of the scattering of light. The same effect can be seen by shining light at an angle through a prism of glass, breaking the light into the colours of the rainbow.

There is one God; yet within this one nature of God, there exists a relationship that none of us can fully understand. God the Father, God the Son and God the Holy Spirit are three distinct 'persons'. Each is fully God and yet they all exist within the character of the one, true God.

The human eye actually sees everything upside down. When light is reflected off an object, it enters your eye through the cornea before travelling through the lens. As it passes through the lens, the reflected image is flipped upside down and projected onto your retina. This upside down image is then transferred to a part of your brain called the visual cortex, which works out what the image should look like and flips it back again.

Test this yourself. Close your eyes, and touch the left side of your left eye while looking in towards your nose. You will see a dark spot appearing at the right of your eye. Now watch the spot move down as your finger moves up!

Just as the light is far more complex than we might first think, comprising all the colours of the rainbow, so the character of God is deeper than we can even imagine.

> In Psalm 119:105, the Bible describes itself as a lamp to shine light onto your path, just as a torch would.
>
> If a person owns a Bible, but never reads it, it is as if they are walking along a dark, unfamiliar road, carrying a torch, but deciding not to switch it on.

Light changes the appearance of everything it touches. As more light is shone onto an object, the colours become stronger, and every detail can be seen on its surface. The Bible teaches in 1 John 1:7 that 'the blood of Jesus Christ His Son cleanseth us from all sin'. When a person trusts Christ to be their Saviour, they are changed. An object will not look the same after light has been shone on it, and neither will a person who has been cleansed with the blood of Jesus Christ.

So light teaches us about God, but light also has a lot to say about ourselves. As we have considered, when a light is switched on in a room, the darkness disappears. Light and dark cannot be in the same place at the same time. If there is light, the darkness has gone; if there is darkness, the light has gone.

The Bible tells us in John 3:19 that 'men loved darkness rather than light'. As a result of the sin of Adam in Genesis 3, all mankind came under the curse of sin. Every future child would be born with this curse, a heart full of sin, a desire to do the wrong thing, to turn away from God and to love darkness rather than light.

For that reason, it is impossible for a heart of sin, a heart of darkness, to know God, because 'God is light, and in Him is no darkness at all' (1 John 1:5). It is only when a person comes to Jesus Christ, the only one who can forgive sin, to have every sin removed from their heart, that the light of God can shine into their life. The wonderful thing about this is that once the light of God has been placed into your life, there is no longer room for darkness. It is only those who are free from the darkness of sin in their hearts that will go to heaven. There may still be times when you will sin, but that will never take away the light of God in your heart.

Not only will we have the light of God in our hearts but, just like any object that receives light, our lives will begin to reflect the light of God. In Matthew 5:14, the Lord Jesus Christ describes His followers as 'the light of the world', since they would reflect the light of God to their family and friends.

In fact, when you think about it, the only way we can see light, and the only way that we can truly know it exists, is because we see it reflecting off the objects around us. With Christ in your heart, your life will be a walking testimony of God's mighty power and salvation, proving the reality of the Bible to all those that you come into contact with.

However, unlike the object receiving the light, which is changed only on the outside, your life will be changed from the inside.

In Genesis 1:4, God divided the light from the darkness. The Bible also speaks of a day when those who have the light of God in their hearts will be divided from those with a heart of sin. That day is coming, and although we are told in Matthew 25:13 that we know neither the day nor hour, we should be ready. We must know that we have the light of God in us, and be sure that we will go to heaven to be with Him.

DAY TWO

> And God said, Let there be a firmament in the midst of the waters, and let it divide the waters from the waters. And God made the firmament, and divided the waters which were under the firmament from the waters which were above the firmament: and it was so. And God called the firmament Heaven. And the evening and the morning were the second day.
>
> Genesis 1: 6-8

Immediately after the earth had been created, it was a place of utter darkness, entirely covered by water. On day one, God had dealt with the darkness by creating light. Now, on day two, He reveals His plan for the water.

Verses 6, 7 and 8 of Genesis chapter 1 describe God raising a body of water that would sit suspended above the earth, creating a gap, a 'firmament' which He called Heaven, between the waters on the earth and the waters above the earth.

Although the terms may seem complicated, the picture, at the end of day two, is clear. Water remained on the surface of the earth, with an expanse of air (the firmament) surrounding the earth. This was surrounded by a further layer, 'the waters above'.

The name Heaven in verse 8 causes some confusion because it is generally understood as the place where God lives. Of course, heaven is where God lives, however, in 2 Corinthians 12:2, this is described as 'the third heaven'. Therefore, there must be two further areas which share this name 'heaven', where one is the atmosphere surrounding the earth, and the other is the vast expanse of the universe beyond it. So in verse 8, the word Heaven simply speaks of the earth's atmosphere, the air that we breathe.

So God placed a body of water above the firmament on day two of creation. However, today, we know that there is no such body of water. Why was it put there, and why is it not there now?

In Genesis 1:31, we read that God 'saw every thing that He had made, and, behold, it was very good'. God's creation was very good, a perfect creation for a perfect man and woman to live in perfect harmony with nature; but it's not like that today. Today, nature itself poses a real threat to mankind, with some of the greatest dangers coming from above the earth.

Burning at 5,500 °C, the sun is the perfect distance from the earth to provide the different seasons, with enough warmth for survival all year round. That warmth, however, comes at a cost, as it brings harmful ultraviolet radiation.

In God's perfect creation of Genesis 1, this necessary ultraviolet heat source could not have been used to harm man or animals on the earth. Therefore, there had to be some kind of protection by which God blocked the harmful radiation, yet maintained the planet's heat levels.

A body of water above the earth would easily keep the ultraviolet radiation at the right level and perfectly trap heat from the sun, without harming God's creation. Here we see the tender care with which God creates the perfect environment for man to live in and enjoy.

Although our environment has since changed, we can be sure that God Himself has not changed.

It is still His desire to care for us with that same tenderness and compassion.

It is that compassion for sinful man that caused Him to send 'His only begotten Son, that whosoever believeth in Him should not perish, but have everlasting life' (John 3:16). It is that same compassion that caused the Father to punish His Son on a cross for the sins of the world. It is the same love which means that if you simply repent of your sin and trust in Christ and His finished work on the cross, you will be free from the punishment of sin forever.

> There are more molecules in a single teaspoon of water than the number of teaspoons of water in the whole of the Pacific Ocean.
>
> Teaspoon of Water = 1.65×10^{23} molecules.
>
> Pacific Ocean = 7.08×10^{17} teaspoons.

So the body of water above the earth shows the Divine care of God for His creation - but where did it go? Why has that sign of care been removed? The simple answer is that it was removed as a result of sin. The sin of Adam and Eve in

Genesis 3 brought a curse upon the earth. Nature would no longer be kind, but now had the potential to bring pain, fear and danger to all mankind.

> The oldest recorded man in the Bible was Methuselah, who died at the age of 969. Methuselah's name actually means 'when he dies, it shall come'. His name was a prophecy from God that judgement would come, almost 1,000 years before it happened.
>
> Methuselah died the same year that the global flood began.
>
> AGED 969

By the time of Genesis chapter 6, the sin of man had become so intense that God told Noah He would send a 'flood of waters' to destroy the whole earth, and that only those inside the ark would be saved. Once again, we see God's tender love as He provides a way of escape from the judgement to come.

As promised, the flood came. The 'windows of heaven were opened' (Genesis 7:11) and the rain began to fall. However, before that day, it wasn't rain that had kept the plants and trees watered on the earth, but the dew each morning. In fact, rain had never yet fallen on the earth. This raises another question: where did the rain come from, and how could there be enough of it to fall for forty days and forty nights (Genesis 7:4)?

Think about Genesis 7:11. The windows of heaven (the firmament) were opened. God allowed the waters, from above the earth, to fall. The sin of man had become so great, that God chose to remove this protection from the harmful rays of the sun, and cause a destructive flood across the whole earth.

Of course, the flood waters eventually settled, and the eight people who had been saved through God's provision of the ark stepped into a completely different world. The firmament had been removed, the land had shifted, the sea water had massively increased and the heat from the sun was now much stronger than before. The sin of man had left its mark, a fact we are still experiencing today.

Before the flood, men were living to an age of around 700-900 years. But now, with the waters above the earth gone, the atmosphere and climate had completely changed. In the genealogies of the Bible we see that each new generation lived shorter lives than the previous one, reaching the current rate of 70-100 years in a relatively short period of time.

It is also likely that this change contributed to the extinction of some of the animals that were on the earth at that time.

Back in God's perfect creation, a perfect protection was given, keeping men and women from pain, from suffering and ultimately from death. It was a blessing from God to man. Even after sin entered into the world, the body of water remained - a sign of God's grace and mercy, even though man had turned his back on God.

However, the protection was only given for a short period of time before it was removed. Likewise, God's grace and mercy to sinners will not last forever. People today are allowed to carry on in their sin, to use the name of God as a swear word, to continue to turn their back on Him, and yet He still offers them salvation through the blood of Jesus Christ.

Just as the day came when the door of the ark was closed and

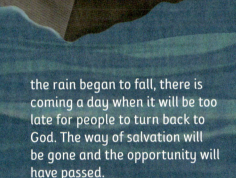

the rain began to fall, there is coming a day when it will be too late for people to turn back to God. The way of salvation will be gone and the opportunity will have passed.

Matthew 24:44 says 'Therefore be ye also ready: for in such an hour as ye think not the Son of man cometh'. God's display of compassion will come to an end, and only those who are found safely in Christ, like the people inside the ark, will be saved. Be ready for that day: put your trust in the Lord Jesus Christ.

DAY THREE

And God said, Let the waters under the heaven be gathered together unto one place, and let the dry land appear: and it was so. And God called the dry land Earth; and the gathering together of the waters called He Seas: and God saw that it was good. And God said, Let the earth bring forth grass, the herb yielding seed, and the fruit tree yielding fruit after his kind, whose seed is in itself, upon the earth: and it was so. And the earth brought forth grass, and herb yielding seed after his kind, and the tree yielding fruit, whose seed was in itself, after his kind: and God saw that it was good. And the evening and the morning were the third day.

Genesis 1: 9-13

Over two thirds of our planet is covered by sea water, gathered together by God on the third day of creation. Today, the oceans and seas are home to millions of creatures, both great and small, but they also play an important role in the earth's heat transport and precipitation systems. These systems are responsible for the different weather patterns required to grow crops and sustain life.

As God gathered the waters together on day three, the dry land appeared. From the shape of the continents today, it would appear that at some point in history, this land was one single mass. The earth's tectonic plate boundaries also indicate that the continents must at one time have been grouped together, therefore we can assume that some major global event must have happened, after the third day of creation, to cause this great 'continental drift'.

In the account of the flood, in Genesis 7:11, the Bible tells us that, as the flood waters fell, 'the fountains of the great deep' were broken up. Water began to rise up through cracks in the land and flood the earth. This global break-up of land, along with the vast amount of water coming through, could easily have caused the continents to drift apart and settle down to form what we have today.

On day three God created 'life' for the first time, beginning with the grass. Not only did this include the grass that covers our lawns and fields, but also the rushes, turf, marshland plants and bamboo. As the main source of food for many of the animals, grass is vital for the survival of life on Earth.

The Lord also created herbs and fruit trees. The word 'herb' refers to all green plants that we see growing out of the soil. In Genesis 1:11, we are told that the herb was 'yielding seed', meaning that the green plants contained the seeds they would need to reproduce.

The highest point on Earth, Mount Everest, stands at a height of 8,850m above sea level. However, if Everest could be lifted up and dropped into the Mariana Trench, the deepest part of the world's oceans, there would still be 2,060m of water left above it, a total depth of almost 7 miles!

These seed-bearing plants were not created to last only for a day, but to produce more and more plants and flowers for us to enjoy. There are as many as 250,000 varieties of seed-bearing plants, making them the most diverse species of vegetation on Earth.

The seeds that are produced come in all different shapes, sizes and colours but they all need the same three things to germinate: oxygen; water; and heat. God's creation was perfectly planned. On day two, God formed the atmosphere, providing plants with the oxygen they would later require. In Genesis 2:6 we read that, although no rain had ever fallen, 'there went up a mist from the earth, and watered the whole face of the ground'.

God had given the plants the perfect amount of oxygen, and the perfect amount of water. The seeds, however, still needed heat, and with no sun until day four, they would not be able to germinate. Therefore, rather than putting the seeds into the ground to grow, the Lord put fully grown plants into the ground first (Genesis 2:5), creating a working world that would immediately appear as if it had been around forever. The seeds could then stay inside the plants until God created the sun to warm the earth, providing them with the exact conditions they needed to germinate.

The trees, created on day three, were also fully grown, producing fruit with seeds that would germinate and grow into more trees. This continuous supply of food would be used to sustain both man and the animals. God did not leave His creation to take care of itself. Just as He does for those who have put their trust in Christ, God showed His care to His creation by providing for every need it had.

The fruit that God provided on day three is still a very important part of our diet, giving us many of the

> There is a parable in Matthew 13 about a man who planted seeds on his land. Some of the seeds found root and grew, while some did not. The seed is like the Gospel of Jesus Christ. Not everyone who hears it will believe in Him.

The Lord Jesus Christ, God's Son, died on the cross of Calvary, shedding His precious blood. He died to take the punishment for our sins. But in 1 Corinthians 15:4, we are told that 'He rose again the third day according to the scriptures'. Christ rose from the dead, proving that He had defeated sin forever, and offering life to all those who would trust in Him.

nutrients and vitamins we need to stay healthy. For example, tomatoes provide Vitamin A, helping eyesight, skin, the immune system and bone development. Oranges and kiwis give us Vitamin C, which strengthens body tissue, bones and teeth. Bananas contain glucose and potassium, boosting energy levels, maintaining blood pressure and helping concentration.

The herbs, plants and fruit, created on day three, were the very beginning of life on Earth. In the New Testament of the Bible we read of another incredible third day.

And God said, Let there be lights in the firmament of the heaven to divide the day from the night; and let them be for signs, and for seasons, and for days, and years: And let them be for lights in the firmament of the heaven to give light upon the earth: and it was so. And God made two great lights; the greater light to rule the day, and the lesser light to rule the night: He made the stars also. And God set them in the firmament of the heaven to give light upon the earth, And to rule over the day and over the night, and to divide the light from the darkness: and God saw that it was good. And the evening and the morning were the fourth day.

Genesis 1: 14-19

It is estimated that there are 100 billion stars in our galaxy and that it is only one of billions of similar galaxies in the universe. Yet the vast number of these stars was only a small part of what God created on day four.

God spoke the words, and by His great power the sun, moon and stars were formed. This included the planets, the galaxies and everything else that can be seen in the universe around us. God set them in the heavens to give light to the earth, and we read in Psalm 19:1 that they show the glory and majesty of God.

God created the sun and moon to divide the day from the night. The sun was to rule over the day, dictating the length of it, and the moon was to rule over the night.

They were created so that we could know the time of day and distinguish between the seasons.

The precise routine of the earth's journey around the sun, as well as its regular rotation on its own axis has enabled us to develop a date and time system. Through this we can calculate the exact hour of a particular day simply by observing the position of the sun in the sky.

As the earth travels around the sun, on a journey that lasts for 365.25 days, the delicate tilt of 23° ensures that the seasonal differences are clearly experienced right across the globe. As the northern hemisphere, tilted towards the sun, experiences summer, the southern hemisphere feels the cold of winter, and vice-versa.

In Genesis 8:22 we are assured that this seasonal cycle will last as long as the earth itself. 'While the earth remaineth, seedtime and harvest, and cold and heat, and summer and winter, and day and night shall not cease.'

The seasons, designed by God, are important, not only to us, but to the birds as well. God has given them an instinctive understanding of the seasons, knowing exactly when they should begin to migrate. 'The stork in the heaven knoweth her appointed times; and the turtle [dove] and the crane and the swallow observe the time of their coming' (Jeremiah 8:7).

Before GPS, travellers used the stars to find their way. Even today, among the desert tribes of Northern Africa, the Tubu people rely on the stars to guide them over the ever-changing sand dunes of the Sahara in search of water.

As well as demonstrating God's mighty power, the creation of the sun was also a sign of the great love that He would show by sending His Son to the earth. In the same way the sun had brought light to the earth, so the birth of the Lord Jesus Christ would bring the 'light of life' to a dark world (John 8:12).

Aside from sending light to the earth, the sun also transmits heat, which is vital for the survival of life. If the sun were to move farther away from the earth, it would become too cold to survive; any closer and we would find it too warm. Even a fractional change in the earth's relative position to the sun could make life on Earth impossible.

The relationship between the earth, the sun, the moon and the stars has been perfectly planned in the wisdom of God to be of benefit to the human race.

For centuries, men and women have been successfully directed through countless journeys on land and sea, with only the stars to guide them - a method which is still in use today. Some have even attempted to use the stars as a guide in their lives, through the practice of astrology. However, as Isaiah 47:13-14 reminds us, the stars can never bring guidance regarding the future. It is only God's Word that can guide in this way.

There have been many attempts to count the number of stars in the universe. However, as technology has advanced, and telescopes have become increasingly more powerful, it has become clear that no man will ever be able to count them all. Yet in Psalm 147:4 we find that God knows exactly how many stars He created, and has even given each one a unique name. And if God cares so much about His stars, how much more does He care for us, who were created 'in His own image' (Genesis 1:27)?

The perfect balance of God's creation is seen again in the placement of the moon on day four. At approximately 240,000 miles from the earth, the magnetic effect of the moon on the earth perfectly controls Earth's ocean tides. If the distance was any greater, the gravitational pull would be too weak, causing the seawater to stagnate. If the distance was less, the gravitational pull would be too large and the earth would flood.

Although the moon gives light to the earth, it does not actually produce any light of its own. Instead, it reflects the light of the sun. In a similar way, a person who has been saved from sin will not shine with their own light, but will reflect the perfect life of the Son, Jesus Christ, in their words and in their actions.

Earth's ocean tides are controlled by the gravitational pull of the moon. After the Flood, God set a limit on these tides, in Psalm 104:9, that they would never again cover the whole earth.

The reflected light of the moon is mostly visible in the darkness of the night, just as the reflected life of a Christian will be clearly seen as they shine for Christ in the sinful darkness of this world. This light, seen in the life of a Christian, is often used to guide others through the danger and darkness of sin to the safety and protection of the Lord Jesus Christ.

DAY FIVE

> And God said, Let the waters bring forth abundantly the moving creature that hath life, and fowl that may fly above the earth in the open firmament of heaven. And God created great whales, and every living creature that moveth, which the waters brought forth abundantly, after their kind, and every winged fowl after his kind: and God saw that it was good. And God blessed them, saying, Be fruitful, and multiply, and fill the waters in the seas, and let fowl multiply in the earth. And the evening and the morning were the fifth day.
>
> Genesis 1: 20-23

Many scientists believe that, over millions of years, some creatures have evolved the ability to fly or to survive under water. Yet in just one day of creation, day five, the Bible tells us that God specifically made both the air and sea creatures.

According to evolution, all forms of life can be traced back, through billions of years, to one cell. From this one cell you, your family, the birds, the fish and everything that you see around you evolved. The problem with this is: where did that first cell come from?

In Genesis chapter 1 we don't have that problem. When God created each creature, He created it fully; each one able to live and function in exactly the way He had intended.

The theory of evolution is in contradiction to what God's Word tells us. God created all the plants, the animals and the humans in only six days. On day five God made all of the birds and other flying creatures.

It is thought today that there are over 10,000 species of birds in the world, with well over 100 billion birds alive at any given time. This clearly shows the magnitude of God's powerful creation.

It was not only today's birds that God created on day five, but also creatures that have since become extinct. Fossil records show evidence of pterodactyls having lived, with a wingspan of up to 12 metres long. These massive reptiles would also have been created on day five. More recently, the dodo, another creation on day five, died out during the 1600s.

It is thought that the earth's oceans hold about 20,000 different species of fish, and God created each one of these on day five. The oceans are also home to a host of other sea dwelling creatures, such as the shark, the dolphin and the whale.

> In 2006, the fossil of a giant 'sea monster' was found, the largest marine reptile ever discovered. In Job 41, an identical creature, with terrifying teeth, scales and smoking nostrils, is described.

It is no coincidence that God speaks a lot about whales in the Bible. Many scientists believe that the whale started out as a land creature and that it evolved into a sea creature over millions of years. Not only is this view against the teaching of the Bible, but it does not even stand up to basic scientific scrutiny.

Imagine the first animal that decided it would like to live in water. It would jump into the ocean, and would die. Then the next animal would do the same, and so on. No matter how much time passed, no land animal would live long enough in the water to develop the functions necessary for survival. Each one would die trying.

Also, the current world record for a person holding their breath under water is 22 minutes, 30 seconds. Evolutionists cannot explain why this would be different for any other land dwelling creature. The answer that God gives is much more reasonable: from His creation the whale has always lived in the sea.

God commanded the air and sea creatures to be fruitful and multiply, a command that they have obeyed until this day. As a result, it is impossible to accurately count the number of creatures that live in the air and sea, not to mention the many undiscovered species that still exist. In Psalm 104:24-25 we read, 'O Lord, how manifold are Thy works! in wisdom hast Thou made them all: the earth is full of Thy riches. So is this great and wide sea, wherein are things creeping innumerable, both small and great beasts'.

Every one of these creatures has been intricately designed by a sovereign Creator. Consider the magnificent eyesight of the birds of prey, or the ability that bats have to navigate using sonar, to see how perfectly designed these creatures are. It is difficult to accept that this range of skills could come from a single cell, but we can believe in a wise and wonderful God who formed these creatures by His mighty power.

In God's perfect design for birds, their eyes can be up to 50% the weight of their entire head, helping them to spot lunch from up to a mile away. The streamlined body of a Peregrine Falcon, for example, can then dive through the air at almost 200mph to catch it.

The Lord Jesus Christ spoke about birds and how they are cared for by their Creator. In Luke chapter 12, we read that the ravens don't grow their food, nor have anywhere to store it, but God ensures that they are well fed. The sparrows are not forgotten about either, and yet God says that those who have trusted in Him for salvation are cared for in a much more wonderful way. 'Even the very hairs of your head are all numbered. Fear not therefore: ye are of more value than many sparrows' (Luke 12:7).

The Lord also used the relationship that a hen has with her chicks to describe the love that He has for His people. We read the Saviour's words in Luke 13:34: 'How often would I have gathered thy children together, as a hen doth gather her brood under her wings, and ye would not!'

The people of that day refused to believe the message of salvation. Today, the Lord Jesus wants you to come to Him to be cared for, like a hen cares for her young. The only way to come to the Lord Jesus is by turning away from your sin, trusting in Christ's death and resurrection, and asking for His forgiveness for all the wrong that you have done.

DAY SIX

And God said, Let the earth bring forth the living creature after his kind, cattle, and creeping thing, and beast of the earth after his kind: and it was so... And God said, Let us make man in our image, after our likeness... So God created man in His own image, in the image of God created He him; male and female created He them... And God saw every thing that He had made, and, behold, it was very good. And the evening and the morning were the sixth day.

Genesis 1: 24-31

The human body is the most extraordinary 'machine' that the world has ever seen. No computer has yet been built that can match the complexity of the brain. No camera can compete with the range and resolution of the eye. No robot can see, hear, smell, taste or touch the way that our bodies can.

The first man, Adam, was created by God on day six from the dust of the ground. The Lord then took a rib from Adam, closed up the wound, and made the first woman, Eve. Of course, Adam didn't have to live with one less rib. Today, we know of a membrane called periosteum that surrounds each rib. So providing the rib is carefully removed, a new one will always grow back in its place.

On the sixth day of creation God also made every creature that lives on land, from the millions of creeping insects to the huge wild beasts. Many of these animals have become extinct, like dinosaurs, but there is plenty of evidence to remind us that they once lived. Books and television tell stories of dinosaurs roaming the earth millions of years ago, but the Bible teaches that God made both man and dinosaurs on the exact same day.

From the many fossils that have been discovered, scientists have created pictures of how these creatures may have looked. They have also invented names for them, like Stegosaurus and Tyrannosaurus Rex.

But long before these scientists were even born, long before the fossils were discovered, the Bible had already given an accurate description of these animals.

Although the word 'dinosaur' does not actually appear in the Bible, the book of Job speaks about a creature called 'behemoth'. Behemoth was a large beast with strength in his loins (hips), and a tail like a strong tree. His bones were as strong as brass and iron. Job 40:19 tells us that behemoth was 'the chief of the ways of God', the greatest of all the animals.

The African elephant is the largest land animal alive today, but this could not be behemoth, as described in Job 40. The skinny tail of an elephant, or that of any other living creature, does not move like a tree. Behemoth must then be a dinosaur, created by God, with man, on day six. 'Behold now behemoth, which I made with thee' (Job 40:15).

The Bible tells us that God designed each animal to reproduce 'after their kind' (Genesis 1:25). In other words, an animal would produce a baby animal of the same species.

An elephant would always produce an elephant, and a sheep would always have a lamb. Of course, there can be multiple breeds within one species, for example when two dogs produce a new breed; however the result is still a dog.

> The cheetah holds the record for the fastest land speed of any animal. With an acceleration greater than that of a Porsche 911, it could run a 100m race over 3 seconds faster than Usain Bolt.

God created a perfectly structured ecosystem, where all of nature obeys His laws, without which everything would fall apart. In the same way, we must obey the law of God in the Bible to avoid the destructive power of sin in our lives. It is God's will that we repent from our sin, and turn to Him for salvation.

When God made the animals, He gave them a natural instinct to gather food, build homes and care for their families. However, He did not give them the ability to solve complex problems and make informed decisions.

These are characteristics of God Himself, and He gave them only to the man and the woman that He had created. 'God created man in His own image, in the image of God created He him; male and female created He them' (Genesis 1:27).

God made man to live and think in a way that animals cannot. With this 'intelligence' we can write books, build machines, produce art and compete in sports. This gives us an authority over the animals, as described in Genesis 1:26. It is a responsibility that we should take seriously, and not use as an excuse to treat animals badly.

When God brought the animals to Adam in Genesis 2:19, Adam showed his care for them by giving each creature a name.

The theory of evolution ignores the authority that God has given by making animals equal with man. The suggestion that we evolved from apes is not only ridiculous, it is also completely against the Word of God.

Humans and animals are different. When God made man, He 'breathed into his nostrils the breath of life; and man became a living soul' (Genesis 2:7). God is eternal, and the soul that exists only inside humans, by the breath of God, is also eternal. One day each of us will die. Our bodies will decay and turn to dust, but the inner soul, the real 'you', will live on forever, facing either everlasting life in heaven or everlasting punishment from God.

After God had made the animals and man on day 6, He created a home for them to live in, the Garden of Eden. The Garden would provide everything that they needed to survive. 'Every tree, in the which is the fruit of a tree yielding seed; to you it shall be for meat' (Genesis 1:29).

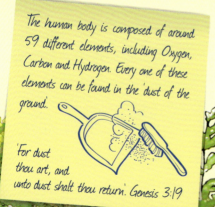

The human body is composed of around 59 different elements, including Oxygen, Carbon and Hydrogen. Every one of these elements can be found in the 'dust of the ground'.

'For dust thou art, and unto dust shalt thou return'. Genesis 3:19

Adam, Eve and all the animals were vegetarian, according to the command of God. Dinosaurs were given no desire to attack humans, and humans would have had no reason to kill any animals.

This all changed when Adam and Eve disobeyed the command of God not to eat of one particular tree in the garden of Eden, the tree of the knowledge of good and evil. Because of their disobedience, sin and death entered the world for the first time, and animals received the desire to kill for food.

Sin had changed the perfect creation of God. The perfect soil now brought forth thorns, the perfect creatures were now a threat and perfect man became a sinner. Adam was separated from God, losing the close relationship that he once had. As a result, every child born after Adam's sin has been born a sinner, separated from God.

Yet even back in the Garden of Eden, God showed His mercy to Adam and Eve, by providing a way back to Himself. The punishment for their sin was death, but when Adam confessed his sin to God, He made them a covering of clothes through the sacrifice of an animal.

The innocent animal had died to provide a covering for their sin so that they could live. As sinners, we deserve to be punished, but we read in Romans 5:8 that 'God commendeth His love toward us, in that, while we were yet sinners, Christ died for us'.

The Lord Jesus Christ died so that we could live. It is not our bodies that will live forever, but our souls that will be saved from eternal death if we trust in Jesus Christ for salvation.

DAY SEVEN

> Thus the heavens and the earth were finished, and all the host of them. And on the seventh day God ended His work which He had made; and He rested on the seventh day from all His work which He had made. And God blessed the seventh day, and sanctified it: because that in it He had rested from all His work which God created and made.
>
> Genesis 2: 1-3

After six days, God had completed His entire work of creation. It did not need to 'evolve' into something else; it was finished. As a sign of that finished work, God rested on the seventh day.

God set the seventh day apart from every other day by sanctifying it. It was to become a special day, known in the Bible as the 'sabbath'. In Exodus 20:8, God commanded His people, the children of Israel, to 'remember the sabbath day, to keep it holy'.

Just as God had rested from His work on the seventh day, so He was commanding His people to take a break from their everyday work, and give their bodies rest. This also gave the people an opportunity to stop and consider the things that God had done for them.

Not only is 'the day of rest' a time when we can remember the Lord, it is also vital for keeping our minds and bodies healthy. According to Mark 2:27, 'the sabbath was made for man'. It was made for our benefit.

The principle of rest can be seen in Honey Bees. Worker bees, which will make around 12 daily trips to and from the hive, travelling a distance of up to 5 km, will survive for about 6 weeks. The queen bee, on the other hand, spends most of her time in the hive, and could live for 4 years.

The human body needs rest. Nothing else will allow our bodies to regain the energy and strength used while we are active. Nothing else can provide the healing, recovery, awareness and concentration that rest brings.

Without rest, even the healthiest of people will become exhausted, and be unable to complete another day of work. If we want a healthy, normal life, then we need rest.

Even when the Lord Jesus lived on the earth, He often brought His disciples into a quiet place to rest, away from the noise and activity of daily life.

God did not just command people to rest, but also the land on which crops are grown. 'Six years thou shalt sow thy field… but in the seventh year shall be a sabbath of rest unto the land' (Leviticus 25:3-4). This principle, known today as 'crop rotation', allows the soil to recover from heavy-feeding crops. The minerals and nutrients are replenished during the year of rest, keeping the soil fertile.

The completion of God's work of creation reminds us of another finished work. After Christ had paid the price for our sins, shedding His blood on the cross, He cried out, 'It is finished' (John 19:30).

The Lord Jesus Christ, the Son of God, had finished the work that He came to do. Through His death and resurrection sinners have been given a way back to God, so that 'whosoever shall call upon the name of the Lord shall be saved' (Romans 10:13).

The Lord rose again from the dead on the first day of the week, the day that we now call Sunday. It was on this day that the churches in the New Testament met together to worship God and to remember the death and resurrection of their Saviour. Nowadays, for that reason, Christians rest from all their work on Sunday, taking time to meet together in churches and consider Christ.

The rest that a Christian experiences, on one day out of every seven, is a symbol of a special rest that will come in the future. Every person who has trusted in Christ alone for salvation can look forward, in expectation, to the day when their life on this earth ends, and they will be with Christ forever in heaven: the eternal rest.

If you have never trusted the Lord Jesus Christ as your Saviour, He invites you, saying 'Come unto Me, all ye that labour and are heavy laden, and I will give you rest' (Matthew 11:28).

7 DAYS

IN THE BEGINNING GOD CREATED

Please contact us with your comments, questions or for more
information on the subject of creation:

info@creationquestions.net
www.creationquestions.net